CROSS POINT ROAD

Cross Point Road

poems

Rodney Nelson

Middle Island Press
2015

Cross Point Road

Copyright © 2015 by Rodney Nelson

ISBN 978-0-6924-4601-0

Published by Middle Island Press
PO Box 354
West Union WV 26456

ACKNOWLEDGMENTS

Absinthe Poetry Review, Arts Pulse, At the Pause, Bumble Jackets, Cossack Review, Coup d'Etat, Cowboy Poetry Press, Cranked Calorie, Epiphany, Flag and Void, Floodwall, Forty-Ounce Bachelors, In Posse Review, Map Literary, On Barcelona, One Trick Pony Review, Open Window, Poem 2 Day, Poetry Pill, Sandstar Review, Scythe Literary Journal, Split Rock Review, Symmetry Pebbles, The Internet is Dead, The Green Door, The Muse India, The Wolf Skin, Tonopah Journal, Tribe, Troubadour 2, Vilas Avenue, Wolftree, Written River, Yes Poetry

A few of these poems appeared in the pamphlet *Late and Later* (Atlantean Publishing, U.K.).

CONTENTS

Cross Point Road

ROMANCE

coming into another valley I would look
for it in a park of finches' mania and
among the new May people
                    American green
              mountains around
and if I had seen it might have
altered my rate of passage but coming into
meant going through and another valley where I
would look for it along a coyote highway
              American brown mountains ahead
                    and in the
tired welcome of a dry October village

I might have seen it there and not gone on to a
winter valley and looked in a crows' retreat or
among a rink of people
                    American white
              mountains above
where I waited to met the eye
of January but young or old went through to
another new valley and more American
mountains
              going and coming
                    on the only trip
in the world for the only reason to take it

BELONG

when there is nothing home to keep you
the road out of prairie to mountain
will open
         take your everyday
to the desert canyon of its map
and it will not be on the coal train
heading east
             magpie and vulture you
have met will meet you again in a
rose-rock country you have wanted but
never seen
       more than a memory
of juniper scent will draw you up
a trail and make you content to live
the morning
            to think with every
dead skunk or woodchuck on the road out
of mountain to prairie how much you
belong to
       you can go home again
when nothing is in it
to keep you

GNOMIC

if I died and went empyrean
I would miss man not only the earth
and want to go back and play in the
music and the idiocy both

if I died and went to Fargo in
winter I would want to return to
earth not man but in July and a
patch of flowering wild bergamot

WAGON MASTER

up in northern wintry Beulahland
women await the wagon master
                are not meant
to get to clinic or
church on their own
           were not put here for
that but to let the wagon master
come and guide or even carry them
over the snow
                lock them inside the
idling heated haven and go on
a road that will dry ahead of him

women up in northern Beulahland
are not meant to be outside at all
           only wait
arthritic at a big
window to give
              not very often
peeps of agony unto the last
doughnut and when not if he comes they
will ride along
           die in a wintry
ditch with a drunken wagon master
on any prairie road beyond them

FLOOD MONITION

at three o'clock on a mild March seventh
I went to the bridge and over to look

in the gray light around and above me
I had to squint now and there were no crows

the top snow layer remained unmarred and
only at the banks had a faint-yellow

pooling gotten onto the ice and it
did not move even though a letout from

a dam or two upstream had made it be
and come from what was running under there

the river was not there that I could see
the one was everywhere that I would

no wind to move pooled water and no crows
at three o'clock on a mild March seventh

THIS CITY

take it with a camera lucida
and one minute of the flood-prairie day
will turn out how

later the unguided
hand may try to put in a hint at fog
but not get a line to the absences

make a mechanical drawing of a
mud pile that used to be snow and the fear
may complete it

figure to trace in black
on white a river coming up the same
or the quiet or the lack of odor

MIGRANT

falcon took a south wind into town
ahead of spring and alit on a
known tower to wait and call and look
for the mate she had not arrived with
               the afternoon
had sun and many
a pigeon in it but she would not
hunt now only go to the ledge she
knew at the top of a high building
and look and call again on the way
               flood water
of mallard she had seen
all morning into town but falcon
went up to the working ledge they would
have not hold and waited and the ledge
I am on is for me never mine

UP

I have not met this spring
but it is another
and will go uncounted

I look at a falcon
or the height of river
and am buoyed anyway

a quick green in the dun
leaf wrack would have me up
for singing and breeding

someone too young may be
waiting at a table
or waiting tables and

ready to take my call
to let me wake again
in the same demimonde

I look at another
uncounted spring and know
I have never met it

HUNTER'S PARK

hawk sticking a home together
that would have to do
            shuttling twig
and branch tip from another tree
to high in the chosen oak
        dry
early open spring without a
leaf to hide its work
            in but the
children not looking up only
a man that did not move this
        mild
day of sunlight on trunk in hawk's
park where robin and
            grackle were
none now and red squirrel few and
April would never come the
        same
nor would the hawk be again or
the watcher only
            some other

REVIEWING GEHENNA

what were you that warm charnel morning
downwind from butchertown when you could
not see through odors of fried pig bone
                     what were you
who in the afternoon
would go to the park and feed on a
woman and give her the meal of you
but a hungry erotic man in
appetite city
              what had you been
in early farm time when to the smell
of cooking pig blood a sausage man
and a sausage woman turned into
vampires behind the granary
                   what had you
been but a gagging child
set to look at a faint photo of
naked bodies in a pit then work
to become erotomaniac
or saintly
              what are you now at the
opening of that pit to take in
butchertown and the charnel farm too
but an old not hungry not holy
man in a county upwind from it

WASH IN THE YARD

do not forget that April morning
with its cabin on the riverbank
                its yard
        and tub of soaped rainwater
the washboard and a working scrub arm

cloud suds were moving too in a blue
that seemed to have paled in the warm wind
                do not
        forget the waving pennant
wash on the line whatever it meant

a skunk had come in the night and gone
leaving an odor mark not a hair
                no owl
        waited in the river grove
or there would have been crows to tell it

do not regret that April morning
though a working scrub arm may be gone
                its board
        and tub are out again now
the crock has sun water for the rinse

FLIGHT OUT OF WHEATLAND

whether they wanted out of the fold or
into another the road between went
up and there were passes in Montana

they saw the heated way of rock and thorn
climbing ahead toward some height that no
mere man and woman in a jalopy

could achieve and where the engine strove they
heard a reproving chant that wanted them
to turn around or strive with each other

alien sky had only sun and a
flight of better people in it and there
were only more passes in Idaho

whether they wanted out the do-and-die
jalopy got them to the other fold
to the tune of rain and strife coming down

and when they headed back to the grain fold
there were no passes in Idaho or
Montana and they went gliding homeward

RENEWAL

spring was love in the morning and a day
of more with apples and Brie and white wine
        affective skin
in the windows' light from
a young garden and the time of it would
keep coming around to the same fountain
          birds chittering
again yet the May would
not slack for two that had acted on it
even when the pebbled walk got longer
        the waking year
tautened a cord in them
and they would not turn from the lilac scent

NONPASTORAL

A lamb could not get born. Ice wind
Out of a downpour dishclout sunrise. The mother
Lay on the mudded slope.

Ted Hughes

Saw a lamb being born.
Saw the shepherd chase and grab a big ewe
And dump her on her side.

Michael Dennis Browne

if I were from mutton country
I would want to carry its ways
into refined maturity
           not the smell
        and only half the
mien of a horny young shepherd
with unforgotten cote or fold
and paddock all in a slot man-
           animal eye to
              fix on the
women in a poetry class
but I am much too wheat-farm to
mimic the waulings of lamb birth
           or tup a
         student in the muck

FOREHEADS ON THE MOVE

even the lost had to take what they owned
       ragbag and child
or child and new valise
and move ahead in an act of resolve
or what appeared to be
                earlier too
they had seemed to march out of the country
as if on willed attack
       not retreating
though no one of them or any knew why

the what and who had made them leave were clear
               not the meaning
so they had only moved
and were determined to do it now with
ragbag and child
       or child and new valise
up the boarding ramp or even the chute
into a cattle truck
            as if an act
of it would bring resolution to them

DOWNTOWN

last night did not become next day
for the drunk yet they have gotten
to a street bench in it where light
hits them early
        why even try
to open an eye when there is
someone or another to cough
and cackle at and stab for half
a smoke later
           why want to keep
the dream of Mount Spokane and a
woman and hard talk in a brain
gone gelatin
        some may make it
to the kitchen at eleven
whether next day be come or not

THE AISLE NOT TAKEN

church high school and the park of its name
were a lawn and more at May's end and
church college did not have to adjoin
to expand the green
                         there and here and
then and now were of good yellow brick
and Bach and to me in my morning
the future would be continuing
with a procession
               in choir robe
or an orientation beanie
on the right walkway to lecture room
or the loft of some neighborhood church
in four-four hymn time
                         music would have
guided me to the only future
but I made out the tableaux
               and turned

AFTER THE NAP

looking up from bassinet
you made a memory of
daytime
        looking up in age
you woke to the light of it
again

but window was a
word and the afternoon had
meaning
        the random clouds had
summer modifying them
as well

which contented you
with being tired in an
armchair
        and seeming alone
with quiet in memory
or now

neither the view nor
the daytime minute belonged
to you

you were every
looker up and there was no
only you and there is not

LATE AND LATER

she knew if I did not what late meant
so we got to the trail on her time

late meant me to listen the better
and to take her slimness in my eye

whether I see her in memory
or some night world of mind's own making

I want to be on that toward trail
or where she turned in parting to smile

she has taken the veil of good sense
and I am in the priesthood of age

but I know that late means later and
will be getting later all the time

JUNE DAYS

seabed prairie did not have the kill
to draw them but vultures were trying
a river park in town
                         seen out in
country next day they rode on high wind
not flapping and I wanted to be
and tear and clean with them
            I am a
turkey vulture at three hundred feet
and as silent looking down for kill
but not of the roadway
                    only time's

CREEK VALLEY

returning to the dew country
might have been waking up in it

that jungly meadow and hillside
might have been home and forgotten

I took the limestone to be mine
and the milk-blue radiant sky

who cared about the rattlesnake
in higher dolomite or what

to call the dewfall bird that went
YEKKO YEKKO YEKKO YEKKO

I remembered in the tent how
one minute lazed into a next

as the JOHNNY JOHNNY JOHNNY
of a woman died out sodden

where the generator came on
the mind of me put march music

but in the easing I had found
who cared about humidity

INDEPENDENCE DAY

parent grackle teaching a young
　　　　　　on the marquee roof
　　　　how to dip
a bread ort in the rain puddle
and the young one making for it
wanting any way

　　　　　　too midget
a cricket on the gravel path
　　　　to jump that high and
　　　　　　too big in
the body and clamant voice a
young crow tagging its provider

to the lecture grove
　　　　how many
human beeves in yard after yard
　　　　　　and not enough crows
　　　　and grackles
and bugs to outeat them maybe

IM GEDENKEN

INGEBORG SCHIPULL † 2003

the tribe had lost the country of pine and lake
                    you were born to
          so you grew up in heather

moved on and on to the end of the West and
                    met me naked
          under public shrubbery

you were winter white but all you said to me
                    looking off was
          the blue of maritime sky

you took the copper words I had made for you
                    mounted them on
          the wood of your dialect

did not however go or stay there with me
                    a hurt that went
          to many more miles alone

and in our age the rainy north where I
                    met you naked
        at a private green refuge

but the dimension you were moving toward
                    one of spirit
        had not kept hex work away

poems did not come up in your flowerbed
                    only shadow
        and it led to the cottage

you were in the dim hex-weighted room with me
                    becoming your
        own memory as you talked

we had been Navajo in another life
                    you said and would
        be together in a next

whatever it was that had worked to take you
                    I do not know
        I am a memory too

FIRST MORNING

everything between the river
and the tree and me came into light
again which movement with the stir of
a nuthatch on a trunk and wind on
water and the water would have made
my first morning paradigmatic
if I had been out there to see it
                    when I walked
into light the color
and smell were too animated and
almost hurt and that first morning would
have been the world's if I had known to
say thank you at or to the moment
which had to come again and again
until I got annoyed in my age
with its seeming frequency but that
morning was a first to me alone
                    a woodchuck
waited at the edge
of the trail ahead and when I moved
it ran into a weed patch making
me want to fall on and devour
as it thought I had come out to do
and why else I had been given the
latitude of another morning
the tree and the river would show in
neither paradigm nor paradise

OLD FORD ON THE TRIBUTARY

the river would have been mill water
with no abandoned car at its side
in the wagon days I think of and
the river would have been meal water

it is heat time in the hinterland
where someone may want to part it out
and me maybe but into what and
it is heat time in the hinder land

PIGEON POINT

the heat intermitted for one warm day
and I rode out in it on the prairie

to where they must have gathered often and
in number to have passed it half their name

they had not come here in a century
and goldfinch had the wooded wet-land now

with meadowlark on the open and sedge
and willow seemed to be waiting but were

in the lull of no man's summer country
and no wind's either for one warm dog day

not anything would go in estrus soon
and I only wanted to find the point

but I was imagining their wings' sound
and would never get to it without them

A WEATHER

come wind and rain in the night somewhere
and blood on the floor of a henhouse

it cannot be an emergency
and the siren will turn or return

another storm in other country
would blow the heat out of any grove

come wind and rain in the night somewhere
and lightning that happens to be now

THE RUN TO QUIVIRA

they did not mention at the starting line
where Quivira would be or what it was
so I ran without any notion of
an objective
      women waylaid me or
the texture of one landscape or another
but every time I wrested me free
and got on my way
          dodging
     feinting to
avoid the next detention until I
hit the tape and went to my knees where the
meditating would begin and they did
not need to tell me more
          I look back now
on my decades' run and wonder at
the Abrahamic zeal I gave to it
     if I had not hurried
          I might not have
   won through
to perfect a hawk's content in
late summer but maybe walking would have
done
         afternoon is ripe in Quivira
   in Quivira
there are no watches here

UNDER THE WILLOWS

no doubt I had set my time for
coming back or around to North
Dakota because I woke up
glad in it
       old enough now not
to mind a wait where to live is
waiting for the conversion of
the world or the big reunion
in Israel or maybe news
of a change
       I'm in a graveyard
under the willow trees only
visiting but would not mind death
much either where it is a mere
continuation of the wait

FRUIT OF THE HEAT

the women were of late summer
where they craned to gather wild plums
in a stuffy dirt aisle between
the grove and tall corn
                    each dark-red
or ripe-yellow fruit was of the
very heat but would go to cook
after pitting anyhow to
make the sweet sweeter
       and why did
the women have to pour new cream
in it that had not even cooled
that added a run of pale fat
to the cloying sauce
                 one hot spoon
would be enough to turn the tongue
and there were flies on the oilcloth
and sweat but the women were of
winter too and would be canning

NOON RISING

I could see it in light of the navy
though it went up and away from water
      the men waited on the wharf
      to get a
bus to the plane and memories of birth
and midnight drill were in the seabag now
         they had emerged on the world
         deck to bright-
gray turret and tower and entered the
command overhead with tinted lenses
      I would see it below the
      tropic on
a vacant white esplanade and again
from prairie that garnered it at sunstead
        but when did I ever see
        it reach the
high midpoint of my own light's only day
between nonentity and nonbeing

AS BEFORE

sand prairie coming wild in
heat and wind of late summer

wild as before with saffron
wave on wave of ripe bluestem

goldenrod moreover in
gyration everywhere

prairie not moving and of
motion awaiting or not

the next ruminant herd and
other bowmen or plowmen

ready as before to take
fire and come wild again

TWICE AT LAKE PEPIN

she did solo pantomime walking in
the water
       a redhead
       white and freckly
and I was undetected up the bank
on impromptu watch
              a dancer I thought
young woman with a fable to enact

I tracked her address and name and we wrote
each other
         the next year
         we sat at night
on her family porch and I DRAW SOME
COMPLIMENTS FOR MY
       OPALESCENCE BUT
THE NAME PLEBEIA WOULD HAVE SUITED ME

I AM NOT QUITE RIGHT IN THE HEAD EITHER
went the gist
       I had no
       dignity and
none to accord so I grabbed and kissed her
anyway but an

                    ill-wisher of mine
would call her up and talk an end to us

I am a dignitary now among
the trees if
                    only trees
                    I carry on
if only with my grizzling or a dream
of Patricia who
        mimed out her fable
to the lake one July to me the next

NEAR CALM

butterflies were in the alfalfa
the alfalfa in a kind of bloom
in a kind of blue and not only
           butterflies
           alfalfa butterflies
underwing yellow when folded up
gold-orange over when extended
in not enough wind and not only
         alfalfa
         butterfly alfalfa
in a kind of bloom on a day too
blue to leave the summertime at in
only wind enough to make a ffff

A NIGHT AT UPPER RED LAKE

I got hiked out so an evening
without campfire would not have done

in the September chill for me who
did not like to have one anytime

I wanted a cabin for the night
but the one I took was against it

the light in the screened porch was dim yet
enough to obliterate dark woods

the walls kept out the continuing
murmuration of big-lake water

in wind but I heard the murmuring
continuation of my own heart

I would rather have listened to wind
on the move in black spruce and alder

the cabin's lighted interior
made me think of a girl I married

who might have called this wood naughty pine
and put on a Bruckner symphony

her awkward wit and okay legs were
only an abstraction in mind now

I would rather have lain with the night
and the bog woods' sphagnum odor and

their creaking and watched the stars and been
in a tent but I was stretching out

in a cabin made against it where
neither sunup nor crow would wake me

HIGH TRAIL ON THE POINT

a one-mile narrow
and wooded ridge to
the point in midlake

but an open trail
in white cedar and
white pine and white spruce

summer coming down
to end among them
and at the water

this walk to open
another without
any name or with

to live on the rock
of the windy point
and be there be here

new moon tonight of
no glorying no
overdefining

TOWN AND FORT

expect not much or demand
when you go to a parade
in the farm town

> eleven
> o'clock is the hour
> of the oaf

observe your mother's
people on the route and do
not say

> but their forenoon is
> getting dogged too and note
> the clothing

polyester-
cotton in pink and white and
sky blue *

> the fort was built to
> invite Indian attack
> be over

and done you think
and what sutler and settler
deeded

       in blood the watchers
       come heir to at this march for
       a redo

the cavalry
were not your mother's people
and the lawns seem tired out

BLUE MOUNDS OF ALL

REMEMBERING FREDERICK MANFRED

I might have watched and listened
at another cottonwood
but I listened and watched at
the one
        at the cottonwood
of all as wind went up and
into its dried leafage and
made a movement and a sound
in it
        another leaf would
come in time where each leaf now
prepared to go but not quite
and would crackle in not the
same wind
        and not the same way
and what I watched and listened
to would never be again
nor would this cottonwood or
other
        a big kid grew up
in the farmland around here
who had the heart and the words
but made him an aerie on
this rock

the red blue of it
not a hutch among the fields
so he was the man of all
during its only time when
he and the rock were fading

ZÓCALO

I must have begun at my origin
to take the incline out of wet night to
the blare of the zócalo
                    must have had
an inclination toward light within
as well and I made it up and onto
the hot flagstones of the Plaza de la
República midway through a decade

        any zócalo
ten years later would
have done and did where a street fair
happened to be in the north and summer
                I must have come
more fully into it
not needing tropical sun anymore
but the next decade I hiked a mountain
range at latitude thirty-five degrees
and met a reflection of true high light
on a magma plaza
                ten thousand feet

TAKING IN

if you dropped a bandanna on the trail
you would turn around in October heat
and find it
                    however remote the spot

would return alone through basswood and pine
you and another had already seen
and get it
                    an item that you had missed

in a remote spot you and another
had already come through but maybe you
unalone
                    had missed like the remaining

yellow at the crown of a tree and would
begin to take in only now that you
were alone
                    even if the quiet there

had not taken you in you would want to
turn and retrace what you and another
of intent

had not really traced even

if the trail did not go only waited
and the quiet of the spot wanted you
to stay there
                    because the other would not

be waiting and you were ready for the
next pond and needed to catch up as if
no one had
                    dropped anything on the trail

FIRE IN THE FALL

they did not want to live in drama
                    even melodrama
and the day
had been hot enough to tire them
already
            they were willing to watch
the drama or melodrama of
where they had slept get charred away and
                    would have been
as willing to have stood
at a victory parade and in
the end to turn home tired as
they did now

only toward shelter
that unknown people were giving them

my own hot day was ordinary
                    beyond enumeration
without
any drama or melodrama
the fire
            breaking in on the day
of other people made me willing
to watch and turn home tired enough
                    in the end

to need no solace and
out on the range a migrant eagle
took a prairie dog while the rest of
the town watched
          only in hiding but
the air went ordinary again

THE QUIET OF NOW

a jeep road into trees
that had been here during
leaf time and were here now

red dragonfly or two
in air the color of
junco even at noon

erupting cattail heads
and through a wickerwork
of branch a wooded hill

in the sun far away
had not been there during
leaf time and was there now

holding out promise and
determination to
the eye in bare gray fall

like one remote headland

the eye had picked out and
set to find long ago

the trees up on the hill
unseen during leaf time
had been there and were there

MAN UPON EARTH

making another Eden in
your mind would have come too easy
given the known and dreamt-up past

but your Haworth of poetry
on the heath had turned out to be
a cesspit village and given

the opportune Americas
you might have imagined Eden
on a mesa or tundra and

not seen the New World ordure that
Kaktovik and Hotevilla
had come to and maybe you would

have tried a condominium
high over Chicago where the
wrong wind did not reach and have meant

to miss the effluvia and
bellowings of rut and heat from
the lots in the Eden stockyard

AND ON

October had been and I soon would have
and the hills I walked in were clear

no green remained to the done field beyond
and some to this tangled meadow

yellow butterflies went ahead of me
and were not too many to count

I took to follow a jig-jagging one
along the way I was headed

until it dove into the tired grass
and would not let me scare it up

its day had been and my own soon would have
and here I went fluttering on

RESIGNATION

the fall has come you thought and were wrong
        it was moving through

        now we are in
the evening of the year you said

were not yet ready to make winter
        its night or end

        and had no name for
the sequential dark beginning in

January even though morning
        of the year would

        have done in that it
started at midnight if not as spring

in fact you wanted winter to be
        termination

you were enjoying
the lesser green and weaker light and

thrilled at your own resignation to
a heated room

with knitted eighteenth-
century cradlesong to hold you

evening snowfall to immure you

NO ONE'S RIVERBANK

I brought in the autumn dandelion crop
with an eye while no one's raft of log and stick
and trashy weed came down the river

early sapient men would not have wanted
a few of anything but I had a mind
to each bent flower and its meaning

they would have swum to it and gotten the raft
idea and then gone on to piracy
and cod hunt and the garbage freighter

no one's hand had made the one-branch prow I saw
and the flowers were ready but not waiting
for the next early men or the last

THE DEAL

if you have talked through time in a building
and done away with more chairs than you know
I may not have what to tell you
                but if
you are out alone when the day is down
without any money or where to go
with credulity intact and you mean
to keep on walking even though you smell
only danger and iodine from the
river
                I may be around to tell you

KENAI STORY

it went running on the howl
toward the cabin
       away
and back again and the two
inside did not need to look
           the depth
       and volume of groan
made it brown bear
           one worried
and remained at the window
staring out in the light night
of June
       at woods no eye could
get through even now that owned
a darkness having to do
with root wad
           tip pit
       more with
what stood
and could see it run
only farther off
           going
then a quick near howl at the
cabin's leeward other side
       the worrier
           just in from

a trip to town
      the other
home all day said nothing on
the hurt rage or who knew what
of the animal
          did not
put aside the magazine
only wondered when the sow
would leave
      when would be safe to
go and find out
          skin that cub

SKILLMAN LANE

red pantiles on a roof across the lane
and Sonoma Mountain unmoving too
but it was time for night now

a bottle of red wine on the table
and a violin concerto playing
but it was time for talk now

we talked and so became other people
and I drove out in the June night alone
to show how it had to be

and none of the other men and women
we looked up to had known one another
and would not even have met

but she had not wanted any of this
to be or have me be any other
she had wanted only me

I turned myself into other people
to cut away from one that loved me more
than who I was could return

an other drove out into the June night
and left a bottle of wine unfinished
the concerto going on

a peacock in a hutch across the lane
and the unseen mountain unmoving too
but it was time for the road

STREET DANCE

and birth got me a ticket to
the foofaraw
                a man among
other men and women who had
all the right
        or was it duty
to party on earth while a band
maintained the old human tempo

and the responsibility
to go away
                I have turned in
my dance ticket but I see a
mountain out there
        and think a part
of me will be with it and is
beyond all of the foofaraw

DÍA DE LOS MUERTOS

it is late in the afternoon of the year
and getting olden and there are many on
the street and you are groggy with relief and
have unzipped your jacket
                          the sun is feebler
but hanging on warm and the tune in your mind
has become faint too
              most of the words are gone
and only LA BONDAD DEL CORAZÓN Y
LA CLARIDAD DE LA CERVEZA have kept
because of one Mexico and its fire
                      you may read them
on the next animated
billboard and not hate the city anymore
only nod having made it to this hour
of a late month
              you are going to rest the
CLARIDAD DEL CORAZÓN Y LA BONDAD
DE LA CERVEZA while the antique leaves in
the air of an oak park are going to rust

¡ADELANTE!

THEM PRIESTS YOU TALK ABOUT
THEY NEVER TOOK A LIFE
overheard in the diocese

the police were not anywhere
but the hundred in the march or
parade did not fear
                    a blue light
on top of an unmarked pickup
of the diocese was winking
at them from the intersection
            moreover
the Kay-of-Cee man
flanked them like a guidon bearer
in carnival pajamas with
a poleax of stick and cardboard-
tinfoil blade
                    even moreover
the crozier moved among them
for noncommunicants to see
and the praying amplified voice
that went with it allowed no doubt
            nasality
did not matter
or the hard pavement or the half-
empty downtown

            the hundred were
on a march or parade that would
bring light to Satan's clinic and
quail the defending host
            the one
that walked with them would raise
the aspergillum and give the
apostate children of Eve a
spritz in the eye if so God willed

A MEMORY OF TODAY

you were moored to a window in
the shallows of winter
              the day
would come full to a vacant sky
any minute and you wanted
whatever sunlight you could get
to make the room its own
          but at
the minute a clouding appeared
that must have hidden in the dim
of predawn and started to turn
carnation only to faint out
when it met the sunup
                and went
on eastering to a point where
the day would have risen ahead
of it
          a watcher have seen and
let the minute in before the
coloration
                and you might well
have been at window moorage there

EARLIER POETS IN MINNESOTA

McGrath in Moorhead looked out for an eye
of knowing glee to match his own and did
not find a one among the listeners
                    not a poetry reading
          anyhow
but an old union singalong

Bly in Mankato wore a Dacron shirt
under his serape and the piping
of a pheasant cock took over the room
                    not a poetry reading
          anyhow
but a self-motivation workshop

Wright in Saint Paul got everybody
to lower their heads with him in regret
while he intoned the rites so weightily
                    not a poetry reading
          anyhow
but a prayer meeting after class

PREVISION

my next time at the tower the army
named devil's a dragonfly will head off
toward some climber on the rock
                        away
from me or not because I may not get
a next and only toward the tower
because the climber may not have made it
        a dragonfly
will be heading I know
toward the rock but not too much up or
away from the grass
                        I know the river
will have a red cutbank next time and the
May scent of it be thick on the trail in
afternoon
        even if I am not there
and a dragonfly will head off away

OVER AGAIN

you have inhabited the room
too long to take it for haven
but today the snow light in it
catches your mind

       as though you were
back from a week on the mountain
and wanted to sit and begin
all over
               needing that now and
you think of an awaited walk
along the ice riverbank
       how
one bad move down there may land you
in the cold to pass with daytime

you sit warm but in another
maybe every other sense
are on that walk or the mountain
ready to go and start over

TIDINGS

had there been an I or not
to slip into my body

what kind of tiding was it

the river the hospital
and a room were what I know

all I do not remember

can imagine the drab of
any midautumn time and

hands at work in the quiet

maybe unquiet dawn or
a nuthatch on the elm trunk

have looked up at the window

there will not be an I to
slip away from my body

just another day tiding

LIMITATIONS OF KIND

your kind do not like to go
to the cities anymore
to watch them teem and fester

you would thrive in daylight at
three ay-em on the Nordkapp
and want to hike all summer

but how to reach it when you
will not even take a plane
and more than one city would

be en route so you may have
to pick another venue
for daylight and three ay-em

say the Brooks Range to which you
could get a ride on a truck
away from the evening

if what you have written earned
you an invitation to

the Riksdag you would decline

because your kind neither fly
nor wear a tie anymore
and do not go to cities

COSMOGONY

rock is what and a rock is a who
but not in mind only in a mind
of a you
            so do not tell or ask
who created it all

what did it

DECEMBER TWENTY-FIVE

I am going out to midwinter
and a day that may equal the scene
of vacant white city and river
      the prairie has invaded again
I may think meaning another term
            snow plain
a day without anyone
to it and in evident need of
the rearranging and adorning
contemporary writers for stage
not to mention page are so good at
      but I do not want
a change out there
only to find mallards again in
the water below the dam even
knowing that more than one duck hawk were
hunting them in summer
         the day will
be all right without a mallard too
or anyone like me but I am
of its coming and going now and
accept each unevent along with
whatever may drop and hit at noon

unclouding had let sunlight downtown
and taken the day beyond its scene
of the morning
                  around the river
new snow that people had not yet tried
to make holy got too white and hid
any mallard track there might have been
at the dam
        this day without mallard

or drop and hit from nowherever
has been an unevent all right if
I do not count the beauty of it

HOME IN A MOMENT

home would have been a hundred
by a hundred miles if the
word had come to meaning
                    no
            particular town or farm
but to go along on a
two-mile ride to a farmyard
in June was home
                    the moment
of arrival in the green
would become the word
            meeting
a cousin to play at the
edge of a hundred by a
hundred miles in the morning

how could home have been more so

LEAVINGS OF THE COLD

January was not a phase
of the country but the country
had to go through what left nothing
to it beyond waiting and work
        to me there was walking too and
        I went out in down and deerskin
        for an aggrieved look at the white
        nature morte of the river woods
        hurrying on before I turned
        into a component
            warming
where a zealot talked at his phone
THE MUSLIMS HAVE INDEMNITUDE
WHILE ME AND YOU AS CHRISTIAN MEN
in some public foyer
        hearing
another at a library
reception desk AND DO YOU KNOW
THEY WENT AND STARTED EARTH DAY ON
THE CENTENNIAL OF LENIN
        when I came home the tap water
        would not get cold to my hand no
        matter how long I ran it and
        I have been in for an hour

ONE WINTER

one childhood winter I lay sick
at home until the fever shrank
into my bedclothing then I
went out to ski in the night I
inhabited
               new snow under
a streetlight on the dead main drag
looked yellow bringing the taste of
medication to my mind and
now the fever inhabited
my longjohns or did I have
a pajama bottom on
        winter
and night were my sickroom and I
wanted to lie down and pick at
the yellow bedclothing of snow
not needing to go inside when
I had night and winter
            day did
not have to come because sunlight
would not have mattered and either
my eye had a tinted lens or
the snow was in an old movie
with Rod Cameron
        but winter
remained immediate and I
had skied out in it weak or not

MORE THAN MILES

even the prairie that knew them
could not keep the young family
together on it
                    so maybe
there would be a home to hold them
in another valley more than
miles ahead
            when they came down and
into it at indeed Sweet Home
a new morning awaited with
an odor of berry field and
the wet sawdust of pine
                    a light
of settlement the family
were not to make their own
            one kid
among them would return to a
flower woman in the garden
of another beginning and
millennium
                    would wait to scent
only another ending and
not let her be a home to him
on the Willamette
            now she is
gone indeed and even that was
many and more than miles ago

FOR SUPERGRINGHITA

FRIEND AND FRIEND'S MATE

that one-night camp in the wind
of the bitter Mojave
would have been too much if you
had not said
          IT'S NOT THAT I'M
          COLD IT'S JUST THAT I'VE NEVER
          BEEN WARM
and at San Miguel
while he and I and you got
turista in that order
you were a beauty and a
New Mexican
      even if
you reverted to brat when
we stayed over at your folks'
          crabby on the rug to look
          at the Sunday paper
      but
you took us up Manzano
Peak with a green felt hat and
were woman not kid laying
into him one rainy dawn
in the Black Hills
          WELL WHAT DO

which led to a
cow farm on the too-green land
that we were driven toward
        for me not yet
and yet it
was the old Supergringo
and you standing up that day
in Dakota March when my
own woman and I married
                coming out to us through a
        wet May in a hut among
hills with what had the label
of Boone Farm on it
                PURE WINE

                DO YOU WANT SOME
        you would not
        have had to ask
heading an
afternoon and night of sweet
rotgut and urination
        a mud morning that numbed to
a word jam you only broke
                IN A WAY
allowing time
to take you and him and me
any somewhere and you have
been tough on your nails I think
        maybe on him

96

though not in
the looks you give the man and
on your sons I do not know
but no greening or flying
or poetry-writing thing
need worry
                    and that same time
          I do know
has kept you a
beauty in the tow of the
Río
                    a New Mexican

WINTER NATIVES

a snow fence to hold out
the winter drifting I
would find north of the grove

I had immigrated
to make a woods shelter
that once seemed big to me

today I would need to
go on a mile to find
the other immigrant

waiting under the snow
in a berry thicket
I cannot see from here

wearing the brown and red
and ringneck of Colchis
without the memory

and I did not learn snow

on fjellbekk or fjordgap
where I have never been

yet we were both ready
and it is the winter
of the pheasant and me

AFTER SCHOOL

the name and numbers of the day
would tell when it came not how
and the afternoon was going
                    a time during
the acorn fall
in a wooded city with leaves
that were turning the color of
oak and elm bark
        warm wind enough
to hurry them down and around
a girl walking into the sun
on the avenue
                    who had stayed
after to play on the wood of
the violin she carried now
and who had a name but many
a number to go
        how she was
in the coloring of that day
would make it belong to ever

YOUNG IN THE CITY

whoever she was and whoever you were
had come into town during an agreement
of time and place
                        found everything so right
you needed to meet to maintain the sunlight
on tree and avenue and the perfect sea
        the Arboretum
and the park it was in
were not enough when you wanted the limbs of
the City and looked up itching whenever
a music or a bean-cake odor got strong
                        hurried even
to read the admonishment
on a church clock tower OBSERVE THE TIME AND
FLY FROM EVIL to the minute you met in
the Tea Garden with Buddha directing you
to a flower thicket
        whoever she was
whoever you were did not maintain a time
a place or anything and you if not she
read another injunction in the green of
the same Arboretum
                        would fly from people

GOT IT GOIN

NINETEEN SEVENTY

you and she were two now but the City
went from COCKTAILS THE HAIGHT and ROD MCKUEN
to MAO REAGAN HARI KRISHNA so
you moved to Brautigan's Noe Valley
                              the Upper Mission
until the morning
sent you on the lead of another out
highway one-oh-one north and it was May
                Round Valley
warm in bloom through Covelo
a narrow pavement and redwood here
and often there into the loco foothills
of Black Butte
                              if you and she had seen an
abandoned ranchería with only
a dome architect and his OLD LADY
getting to work you might have pulled over
because you were communitarian
in vocabulary
                to that extent
and maybe not so would have driven on
as you did to the radio's song YOU
GOTTA GOOD THING GOIN
                              a dairy ad
meant for the ear of the cow that you saw

by your ascending way to the very
Eden that a missionary pilgrim
would have chanted in dreams
                at a tent site
on Mendocino Pass you fulfilled the
mission to the extent of reckoning
you were man and woman not what it was
or where the road led
                            anyhow you did
not have to take one-oh-one forever
down to the City of America

WRITTEN TO A WOMAN FRIEND

you have traveled to more
of the imperium
than many another

your mind learned to fly in
the wheat country that was
an airpark for leaving

you let no craven word
in the town or later
set you a boundary

yet you as well were taught
about the enemies
of the imperium

who are to be chocked and
you wear a uniform
no one can see so why

not board a flight to meet
a warrior in snow

heeding reveille at

an elevation and
give a pointed laugh
and take uncertainty

when you carry a map
of the imperium
in your overnight bag

WALK BY NIGHT

in my eighteenth May I was up
all night to read and smoke and in
the predawn I went out to walk
the rest of it
      worms were many
on the cement and akin to
the wet-grass odor with robins
starting to talk
   my mind wanted
the morning too as my body
got heavier and at sunlight
the notion of a poem took
me home
     the words coming quickly
   WAS IT THE DOUBLE OF MY DREAM
    THE WOMAN THAT BY ME LAY
    DREAMED OR DID WE
to balk right there
     part the dream
    or each take a part
of it I did not know although
another line waited ready
    UNDER THE FIRST COLD GLEAM OF DAY
and the next I knew it was noon
    too bright and humid
to go out

or think of what I had written
so I opened Yeats' collected
to my very own lines and blinked
and read them again
       there had been
no dream and no woman other
than a junk-shop Aphrodite
on my table and with feeling
           no awareness
       no malintent
I had taken the lines and tried
to make my own poem of them
          noting that Yeats'
deft way out of
the snag OR DID WE HALVE A DREAM
seemed not right meant very little
to a kid with only the ash
of emotion left in him now
and I laid it all to fatigue
       or had
another walked with me
on the damp avenues by night
         maybe
when the living are dumb
or reticent a ghost will come

NIGHT TRANSIT

I do not walk out into the dark
but now I have to
                it is a mile
from one heated point to another
going over a bridge and next to
the river park and through downtown on
a Friday night
        love got me into
a world that turned out to be war and
I need a hard mind to survive so
I am marching ramrod
               not walking
and on a patrol not an outing
by order of my unnamed command
        if I falter
or seem to I may
not make it to the warm apartment
that awaits me like a sentry box
or guard tower
               I am at the start
of a weekend yet no one is out
on foot and not many driving to
remind me
        so what did I expect
            a northern city
goes empty with

winter and rigid and so do I
ignoring the relaxation of
the pine trees here and what did I think
to see
      enemy in camouflage
          the night
is a baffle to my drum

RETREAT FROM THE WILLAMETTE

a family I knew began to go apart
when mother and daughter moved to Cascadia
   dark little mountain hamlet
   of woe in the rain oh woe

father and son remained at what was left of home
and in the bowling alley no one had to talk
and the river was up and had to get higher
but what did it have to do with the family
who reunited every weekend in a
   dark little mountain hamlet
   of woe in the rain oh woe

a Mormon-redneck town or just redneck-Mormon
of work and no chatter where the pine trees were high
and still growing on yew-ess twenty all the way
and the family had nothing to add either
as they waited out the fall of Sunday in that
   dark little mountain hamlet
   of woe in the rain oh woe

TUTORIAL ON THE PLAINS

take the road west without a gee or haw
to find the wilder up and down of it

come to light in a field beyond reason
and know what hard wheat is along that way

no need of roping calves or anyone
to get man-sweaty where the tractors bawl

take it east to the university
and be on the road to deconstruction

ARISE

when you woke young in the tent and morning
and spring with a memory of the wine
and love that had made your night you could see
all the redwood arriving and wanted
to join the whiskey jack on a picnic

when you woke old and alone in the tent
and morning and spring with no memory
of love or wine or the night you could see
the lake sky widen and wanted to join
the crow or were there two on a picnic

PROSPICE

the desert plateau you took to
without qualm or resignation
you would leave for the home prairie

       what qualms were there were there

you had no need in rain and flood
to water the roots of you and
be prebendary of one plot

you have a need not to resign
to any one sky or country
and would walk the plateau again

       what qualms there are there are

SPRING MORNING IN WINTER COUNTRY

five degrees I read in the predawn
but the heat did not come on
                late March
in winter country and the dial
was set to fifty-five overnight
      had been
during January too
when a reading of five out there at
the same point of morning not hour
would have made it tick into action
              where sunup
would be was going red
in not a sky of winter at all
and the thermometer went to three
but the heat did not come on
      maybe
predawn hinted at a greater light
than January's to come and the
sensor picked that up the way I had
even though it was said to react
to temperature changes only
           no warming
of direct sun yet in
the room which did not in fact need it
and nothing wrong with the thermostat
      I had heard

the tick of heat at three
or so and now I ran a check on
the overnight readings
                    it had been
eight degrees above at that hour

IMPROMPTU ON A LINE

NO SPRING CAN FOLLOW PAST MERIDIAN
—Wallace Stevens

I am past the meridian
of my moment but there is more
        the moment
that my own is in
and I have been a hunter on
the track to its every reach
                a pilgrim
circuiting the lands
of it over and over and
making them all that I wanted
        if I had not
gotten out and
around I would not have become
a scratch poet where I am now
beyond meridian
                or seen
the spring beginning to follow
anyway in the river of
my moment and it is but there
is more
        to take another round
of all the many lands within
my keep on the circuit

maybe

helix

    I have been traveling

ONLY NOW

I had driven half a night to
the stewed edge of Oregon but
the tidepool air took my breathing
away
      right and then I hit out
for the desert not knowing what
had happened earlier that year
in Oregon
         not thinking of
someone I had ridden with on
the beach highway only the air
I needed
      which I found when I
went through a town I could not name
having driven another night
         Barstool California I
heard a man say at a truckstop
and right and then I got to where
I wanted
      a way out of wet
and dark to the intaglios
that other ancient unknown men
had cut in the desert
       not right
and then but on a day that had
to come I learned of her dying

in the stewed Oregon she had
come to
      it is only just and
now however that I put when
she left next to the date of my
waking to a pleuritic gray
and note the so few months between
        who had
not meant to keep me in
our younger time thought again
on an ocean-highway ride
in our age
      right and then was
too late and I did not regret
one more parting
        only just and
now do I wonder what it was
after my half night on the road
that had me take a sidetrip to
the tidepool edge
     of Oregon

WORKADAY RIVER

the river went to flood a time
too many for hyperbole
and what I thought it sang
                    OKAY
            LET'S GET AROLLIN'
seemed tired

even children live in the gray
between the word of what they have
to do and the doing
                    OKAY
            LET'S GET AROLLIN'
they singsong

Buddha and Jesus gave color
to the moment relieving it
of tedium awhile
                    OKAY
            LET'S GET AROLLIN'
people hummed

I heard a hymn to the comforts
of workaday routine in the

moving gray distension

OKAY

LET'S GET AROLLIN'

of water

THE SEA'S LAND

the sea gave way to prairie
before you came to name it

you farmed and bred in your time
heeding the words of a book

the prairie had so much room
winter could not deject you

and April gave so much light
you joyrode out to the field

now floodwaters are taking
all the land you are known to

no matter how deep the ditch
you make or how high the dike

the prairie is giving way
and the sea will come again

you will not be here to find
a name in the book for it

PASCHAL

and holy week another to wait
out mud and snow and the going down
of floodwater
                    you have ridden through
as dim an April in high country
but here the river is wrong for a
maundy washing of feet
          too risen
and cold so how will you ever go
to commemorate the beginning
of the wait
                    and millions have been
at it for millennia and the
watchlights of Yerushalayim and
la Città di Vaticano are
burning on
          a holy weekend of
mud and snow and flood will have to do
even if you are bowlegged and
-minded already
                    from the weighting

FULL NOON

our young time filled out where the park came
with windmill and tulip garden onto
the native beach
                    the forward innocence
of her look in our day nest among
the shrubbery meant she did not detect
the impostor in me
        a man was taught
to wive and sire and found under law
and in the full of our time I did
not see either
                    she would and so would act
that I was one for the moment only
and every word it had to give me
owning no other home
        our noon at
the beach or later in rooms ended on
the telephone and she would die alone
in our age
                    I have had decades of
moment to weigh the why of her and what
I did not seem to be and was and I accept
and wonder
        how would she have looked
turning to me where our time filled out
to the tune of the sea if I had been
another

the man I saw reflected
in her innocence and tried to become

DITTY

the falcons had come in March
along with high water

it did not want to be spring
whatever it had been

the water was not leaving
but the falcons were here

and every turn of wing
said die to a pigeon

the cold earth and its layer
had to give up to sun

but snow of an April night
made any change away

it did not want to be spring
only to make away

whatever it seemed to be
whatever it had been

GONE TO THE ANIMAL

you remember the May you went
on a steeplechase of one to
the Jim River valley
                    before
your age of commentary the
bustle and flounce you were hunting
            you do
and would not have to wait
or pray in rage again because
every hill you saw had a
new green
                        you remember riding
out of the tallow you had been
and into buffalo meadows
that sunlight made open
            you do
with bustle and flounce and your age
of commentary gone because
it was only the buffalo
you were hunting
                        now you take on
the very expression of one
the deliberativeness too

MARGINAL SPRING

another spring of high river
and floodplain going to tideland

two weeks' wait at a midtrunk height
of water in the elder grove

the warm air in a vacancy
with no arrival wind or birds

catkin turning to leaf somehow
but green only at the margin

to write and make a life in the
geoponic words of floodplain

to invent a new one in the
hydroponic words of tideland

another spring of high water
and quiet in the elder grove

to be up to your trunk in it
trying to bud out at ebb time

CITY NIGHTS

she was a daughter of the house
on El Camino del Mar where
I did not exist
                    an import
from the Mediterranean
where spice had turned into perfume
and resin into the gems of
a hidden garden
            from Munich
along her way to another
coast of sun and pomegranate
                    to be home
at twenty in the
doting house that let her hide me
a night or two in all the need
and confusion of her high room
            where I
did not exist on El
Camino del Mar
                    not longer

MAY SLACK

thirty finches of the same yellow
do not remember brutality
when they feed on sunflower nut in
the tree garden
                    it is only May
and someone tore open a bag and
their sound of overjoy is infant
or idiot to me though I am
watching them
            beauty was mine to be
one time and a minute all that I
got to mate in and she dried into
a wise woman
                    dying any and
every way and all I got was
wise to nature
            the brutality
and the finches do not remember
in May slack and I look and think of
tornado and meteor
                    flood
        quake
not however unaware of the
honeysuckle ready to flower
and I can give up to overjoy
                    I can chitter

like a moron too
and feed on nonremembering
     a
finch in the killer wind on its day
and a finch in the tree garden are
the same and maybe I can be one
during the impersonal jerk of
the great quake
          take it as an earth shrug

THE DAY AFTER MARATHON

something had pended in them and
they ran and let it out to win
a day of recovery
        but
it was mid-May and we could see
from the deck that something pended
on the river
              in the sky too
and why did the bright overcast
make the green darker
        more intense
we might have wondered looking at
a world that never went inside
where many of the marathon
were recovering
              rain did come
but only as the envoy of
a tornado eight hundred miles
away
        and we talked about the
befallen and the misfallen
and what awaited
            did not probe
the unshared or unacknowledged
or run inside only went when
the bright intensified making

the rain harder
          not quite enough
to let out what pended in it

MAKING WARM

the May gave only more brown floodwater
and ended in a tree-outrooting wind
and you took it
                        disremembering where
you used to go in better hill country

but say you walked into the next day on
a lake beach and the immediate note
of oriole
                        sight too and dragonflies
more than might have been along a dream road

would you remember how to take the sun
and one loon cry on a midafternoon
beyond the May
                        let it make warm of you
in the same hill country of the minute

THE CAPTIVE STYLE

why anyone would want to hold
a man like me in Babylon
I do not know but writing in
captivity gave me a style

which I outgrew and now I laugh
to see the trickery of it
in what the others write although
not one of them was held with me

I have been out for twenty years
and publishing so it could be
they learned my early captive style
from how I wrote on my return

why anyone would imitate
the rhetoric of Babylon
I do not know who often saw
what hanging gardens really meant

THE VILLAGE PART OF A TIME

it took up more of my childhood than
any other site did or would do
and included my friends wielding spade
and rock to kill a gopher and one
late-March day when the melt had exposed
the droppings of winter and town and
town dump looked much the same even if
the geese were dinning north
                            but also
the heavy summer green that a hand
had planted and the cut weeds' stink where
a man worked his scythe into what had
grown wild out of hand and peppery
leaf smoke in autumn which included
a friend's old dog killing an old tom
and then holy wax on a wood pew
during the indoor months
            how can I
declaim the loss of the morning when
we wonderers were turned out into
a fenced prairie tract or of a time
not over yet that has come around
indirectly and gathering up
the histories of all I am now
to my later better site in it
as if the town had told
                        what would be

PONY BOY

a March night on Lake Havasu
and you could hear the children sing

they might have been too old to talk
for all the words you understood

but Pony Boy in the refrain
did make it over to your camp

the name of some unknown maybe
who had not wanted more than that

who had not earned what he came to
along the road in a red gulch

the love you find has never been
a part of any other thing

and you had hobbled onto it
in such a way as he had done

they sang of Pony Boy and you
for that one step along the road

CROSS POINT ROAD

the days in the lake region that year
were of honey
          the nights of water
                    only wine
between us and we drank
from a bota in the car
                    you told
me to stop at the Round House Inn on
the turn to my cottage but I laughed
          we wound up arguing
in a park and I can remember
the fireflies
          there has never been
a Round House Inn at Cross Point Road but
I have made the turn
                    am driving it
                    too late
          in another July and
water night to find you where I
have never had a cottage or been

GRASSLAND

who would want to be on mud prairie
in August
               heave both legs through gumbo
and heat under no eye in the sky

the too-bright earlier greens have an
effect of immaturity now
and only pothole water ages

river and mind are glutted but find
no outlet
               wait in a crampédness
for sunlight to evaporate them

no one imagined that red clover
blooming on wet sand prairie would have
to do with anything one wanted

WORD PAINTING

shouldn't nature be apprehensible
in itself
needing no commentary at all
only description
shouldn't mere narration be enough
NOVALIS

that is what we might have thought
on a certain afternoon
of childhood when the party
got bad
the men were drinking
and yelling and wrestling in
the farmyard and we wanted
to be unheard and unseen

we were not ready to think
only to run to haven
in the deep pungency of
the grove
nature was a boon
to our primitive mind
which would not forget the late-
summer green inviting us

a flat description of it
may sit well but when we write
that party at the farm is
still there
                what we recall of
the grove cannot mute out the
violence and narrating
nature is commentary

RED LAKE CATCH

morning was up again but not your time
and you might have been twenty on the pale-
sand edge of that huge lake
        ready to take
and do and launch whatever boat into
the mild white-capped water
                pay out the net
or lines and bring in the catch and sell it
then go to love or war
        your tongue had not
forgotten the beer of that August and
you had known even then where it would lead
but connecting the two had not mattered
                now you
were looking back at the high pines
the too-loud forest green of which on blue
you must have been making up in your eye
        walking too easy
for an old whittler
when you caught a thought or a thought caught you

young is being able to crick your head
around enough to see what is waiting
to take and do
                that was all you had been

LOOKING

daydreaming back not looking
you seem to see a bay
of clouds and wind in childhood but you
do not smell it

imagining ahead not looking
you seem to see
the daylight in the canyons of your end
not feel it

looking not daydreaming back
you see not seem to where
the walk you wanted has come into
the park and is

looking not imagining ahead
you see where you
are going among the faint-scented oak
and will be

WINTER FOG

and fog and even more of it
to end the afternoon has made
the February day a place
not to wait in rather to be

the moment is more where than when
so gather it letting the rain
of Decoration Day await
another place not a better

birds may be hiding already
in the air of the avenue
with fog and even more of it
to start the February night

AMERICAN RADIO

I do not have the embouchure
to blow an ivory horn and
Roncesvalles Colorado
is not a gig on any map

a bellying of cloud in sun
may make me want to go out there
but never Corbenic Utah
to find what everyone found

you are the only one and what
I have been looking for as were
the young dead armored horsemen of
another self-benighted time

if once or again I met you
I would yell montjoie with reason
and we would fly and sing away
on American radio

RUMBLE STRIP

who called life a journey or a dream
had the mind of a ballerino
and to me it is more definite

a numbered route through Colorado
like yu-ess fifty and not one-way
or straight but an ambient to get

from truck stop to truck stop on the clock
and that is what I have driven though
I sooner would have ridden shotgun

laughing in and to and at the sideview
mirror to the very canyon rim
where I would have imagined the head

of an old man of rock in profile
his squint and attendant toothy gawk
been ready to see myself in him

the definite road is not all mine
so I can yawn knowing there will be
a rumble strip ahead of the end

UP THE COAST

a branch overhanging the cold water
of the inlet and a cat on it in
the only sunlight to win out over
late March and the cold rain
                        Sinclair Inlet
but why the derivative name Sinclair
not Saint Clair
            why so hard to forget a
tableau of cat enjoying sun on branch
and why tell it
                        or of the young smiling
redneck mother and wife who wanted to
talk in the next cabin when he was not
around even though you had a woman
            prettier
in your own and why hard to
forget her anecdote about a mad
prefesser drownding in some pool over
on Bainbridge
                        a pine-backwater accent
or of the whole coast wakening out of
immersion into light and warm with cat
and everyone in easier green
on an inlet becoming the saint's own
            hard to forget
the cat was hers
                        why tell

150

CHILDHOOD AND AGE

they took you to the library
in the morning where a woman
mentioned the stacks and your mind ran
out to a field
                    each one of them
of hay and like a town building
but not close enough to the next

you returned to the library
that evening where a woman
mentioned the stacks and your mind ran
to the desert
                    each laccolith
a high independent hoodoo
in a cracked pink field of others

WHEN AND WHERE TO BE

who but studs of another world
would have shot pool too late at night
on the Fillmore
           gone babbling through
the city's manic monolog
not thinking to be heard or seen
in the bottom right-hand corner
of a news photo
                Molly's tits
got her a job in North Beach while
they tried to take John's camera
in the Haight
           beard or not
Gary
ran out to Chain of Lakes to pray
with a trombone while Connie in
the Mission did not make coffee
until noon
                Warren and Rodney
went babbling to Hippie Hill where
someone not yet Janis to them
had a flatbed truck and a group
and a song
           it did not matter
who had written the ticket to
incomprehensibility

everyone got there on such
a rhododendron day
                    seeing
the sun through wine or such a too-
late night of foghorn and beancake
in what but not another world

NEEDING OUT

Greatgrandpa would have taken
the flare of white that met him
at the storm door with a squint
and headed out into the
unkind wind of early March
needing to see to the farm

I have tinted lenses but
to me the new snow is too-
bright chalk and the wind will put
an ache on my bad shoulder
making me want to be in
not out of the apartment

I have dreamt of Theresa
a meeting in another
arrondissement even though
I think it will not happen
and I would rather sit here
and speculate about it

Greatgrandpa would have limped out
to do what had to be done

taken the pain and knowing
of his way will be enough
to get me past the door and
on the street in a minute

AND YOU COULD HAVE

if you had died at twenty-six that night
        in a beer ad
it would have happened in
San Mateo
             if you had died that day
it would have been in a toothpaste ad at
an eatery
      the parking lot
        the car
that hit you and the motor scooter you
were on would have been the same
      either way
and you would have seemed to dive right into
a palm tree
          you might have been the rider
or riding with
      the friend might have been John
or Sandra of half-Greek half-Swedish looks
trying to follow you into the air
        whichever the time and ad
      either way
but you see only you
        a green sport coat
out of motion at the palm's foot
      too young
and smug to have gone at it with your head

and wait in sun- or floodlight quite like that
at twenty-six
             your grin becoming wrong
when they take and heft you but the ad shoot
would have been inside of the eatery
        the crew would have heard
             not seen

THINKING TO FIND

winter beginning late did not go on
and March has taken the snow of the park
leaving it open

I looked for you in the brown park I wrote
one time about another I thought and
I did not go on

there were a robin and a grackle out
I wanted to include but here I see
no activation

if there has been no word of spring how can
it happen I am thinking now at the
side of a willow

I doubted you were in that other park
and know you're not in this but I go on
looking anyway

SUMMER WIND IN MARCH

the dry winter would end in a flood
of south wind and the river was up
not much
            moving quick but I might not
have seen if there had not been coming
an ice load from a tributary
in remote woodland
      the water here
had none in it yesterday and in
the park no gray drift remained to melt
for the cresting
            only an hour
ago I was out on the bank and
the river may be down already

IF I DID

if I went into town today
an older man would look at me
with dog eyes
            not at what or who
I am or was and I would find
more pathos in a wooden bench
than drollery
      next to a store
that few remember open and
in the grain of it I would see
a carven heart
            the love of men
and women seemed to be only
a soldiering on to the kid
I was
      maybe am
            yet a hand
had cut what did not have to do
with field expostulation or
maneuver into it
      and if
I were to go to town today
I would meet the dog eyes of an
origine
            who used to sit
on a bench that few remember

THE MAMELUNDS

let me be old a minute and write
about the Mamelunds of inland
Norway one son of whom made it out
    too many mouths and no means
        going
not in pursuit of an absolute
to America but fleeing one
I come to think
    one that limited
his reach to a bounded town and the
immediate woody hill
        getting
to rig a farm above the valley
of the Sheyenne River in dark earth
and the green shale of which I have a
minor hunk on my counter
    dying
with an only son before dust came
and those he'd left had to make it out
    too many mouths and no rain
        going
not in pursuit of an absolute
to the Northwest but fleeing one I
have come to think
    one that limited
their reach to an empty fork and the

immediate dry pasture but they
took it along
       from Norway
  from the
Sheyenne valley and would not have had
to get on out at all
      only up
I am thinking but let me be young
a minute and remember no one

CRACK OF SPRING

the winter was too mild to end
and the warm went on increasing
and did not make it to a change

got set back after equinox
turning into advertisements
for a time I would have to earn

but I met a vigor wind today
and saw an allusion to green
on the turf and in the river

it was under the bridge I felt
the warm become more than promise
and change into the crack of spring

PLAINS SPRING ABOVE THE DAM

you woke to that country in its April
and your own
                        the rawhidey hills turning
more and more Indian the higher an
arm of the slackwater got
            taking towns
in the bottomland that were not your own
and even the dry wind was becoming
a matter of girl
                        spring coloration
arriving in cut time and half note but
slow and you would like to walk on the dirt
of that country again if not relive
that April

            the road to the bridge was closed

UNSHADY GROVE

        a drawn-out early spring
in the known world
    the only

no birdsong yet
    the quiet
        and not a word from me

    it is April
        for the winter nuthatch
I'm a groundling

        in a one known world
of catkin
    not leaf

STEWERSHIP

and the place is no longer ours
DHL

heat cabbage in a pot of cleanser
to make the right chemical stew and
serve it tomorrow with a side plate
of burnt-out mineral garbage

you will need to be an it creature
to eat the earth you're on and survive
with an omnifarious diet
the oven never going out

the arm that you got amputated
did not belong to you anyhow
and letting go the earth will not hurt
if you are its main infection

Robinson Jeffers had to inveigh
and Edward Abbey to laugh when they
spotted what you were turning into
but the ears on you went foreign

THREE OF THE WEST

GARY ELDER
BILL HOTCHKISS
LEN FULTON

I rode with one of the men to meet
another on the Sacramento
and the trailers of winter rain cloud
were smoke to me
    and up the valley
into the foothills to see a third
at a compound of wood smoke and in
a week I would think to kill myself
        and among
big metacowboy men
of the West were Elder and Hotchkiss
and Fulton and easy toward one
another and with me
    if not the
America behind the rains of
nineteen seventy-nine and I saw
the two that only time
        the winter
I rode a truck with one and watched and
listened to who were men of the pen
and older than I and had done more
with all givens

                    and in a week I
would think to go to Coronado
and kill myself and did not and of
the winter three
                    no one's on the bay
or the river or in the foothills
and I the living am elsewhere but
the California part of me
is wondering what they will write next
        not thinking
of Coronado Bridge

TAKE IT

the way you see you doing and being
in every detail with a woman
at the sea would make you want to relive
that afternoon
        but once you got to there
and then it would not seem any shorter
than a rainy April one in the land
around you
    and the you that you see was
an arbitrary recombination
that might have put you in a baboon troop
during the age of Thoth or let you do
and be as a gnat
        your one long summer
an incomparability not to
remember whether it had flown away
in the Permian
    or at a green lake
of nineteen ninety-nine but you need not
relive a sea or woman or the arms
of a babuina
        when and where and what
you were and might have been is all you are

BLOWING RAIN

honeysuckle in bloom
next to a door that might
have been open to me
on a milder morning

and the nectaries of
the mind in action too
but not quite sending out
a word or anything

wind too crude and wet on
this side of April and
my own unheartiness
under the flowering

VACANT FARMSTEAD IN SPRING

dandelion and fritillary
are out in color and I hear wrens
and walk on the maturing green to
alfalfa acres that have become
a matter of tall dead gray plant stalk

and the moment is of the farm not
including who were here and me and
even though I am on and of it
I look at the grove and buildings as
if they were in diorama

I am part of May everywhere
and would not have to be at this farm
where my mind and eye are not drawn to
any leafings but only return
to the plant stalk of another year

ENVOI

going into the death room will not
remit a nine-month distance in more
than time or make a window light I
have known seem less unfamiliar
in the odor of Rodentia

PEOPLE PARK

May has taken the light to greatness
and the cabbage white is free to jig

but there are no more unguarded days
no matter who wanted to have one

saying GLORIA to the river
would come off as ridicule and make

the morning jogger drop to one knee
with a look of indigestion and

who got along and around and by
so long are writing NON PLUS to it

that redwood outbuildings adjoined to make
one side of the pebbled ranch yard I knew
and must have come late in the day
    because
I did not get to awareness until
I went inside
        the father touring me
without a word and the daughter and the
granddaughter following in a silence
that welcomed me
    a cat appearing too
I had named Knutsen held no rancor and
I felt my marriage to the daughter had
not ended in hard hurt after all but
my stepchild did not talk
        only pointed
along with my father-in-law to show
how all the outbuildings had been gutted
    the shop and the garage
        and the cabin
the walls taken out and I noticed a
wine stain on what had been my work table
so they took me to a solarium
    new but unclean
that looked out on a field
of adobe earth where I had tended

and irrigated my peppers
                touring
me back to the half-lit garage and I
sank to the dirt floor in the knowledge that
not one of them was older
        that my wife
of one bright ridden time had lipstick on
and I had not been so sad in a dream

HERON AT FELTON PRAIRIE

arriving at upland
you take its weight to you
with another eye on
the contour
   the heron
 green or black
soloing
around the pothole and
you are a gauge of the
water in it
   an eye
 among
wood betony
for the prairie's moment
where every live thing
of any time has come
to agree
   you would have
no other gods before
that heron
 black or green
winging around in the
roomy day but not off

TRAVELOG

one look at that height of cloud in sun
and you drove out to where it would be
thinking how many the forms a cloud
would have taken on in the times of
how many changing men and women

and at the side of the way were bunched
the forward young greens you expected
while on the road you went in a din
of iron and glass among the few
surviving droplets of a virga

the cloud rock where you tented was part
of the hard and glinting too and down
in the river valley other men
and women were bunched to fornicate
and fuss and fight the green time away

you thought how many forms a mountain
would have taken on in the moment
your trek to the mesa top began
of how a same changing might get you
at a wrecked cairn and no more slowly

but you were pathmaker not -finder
did not have to read a given in
the faces or call a place other
when you were so few among any
in country where you had always been

WILD IRIS

I convoked the flowers in garden
and took the name of every one
on the trail with me
               intending to
hike it out of my age and be mock-
sententious when I ever got to
the top
     for all times' sake
               but what I
walked through on the pine mesa did not
await any name and I could tell
these iris were not in mind

     flowers
had been garden had been memory
of a setting
               not untame like these

ONE WAY TO SEE IT

and you have been a pilgrim to
the drab river you were born on
and now they want to dam and shunt
the water into their own course
making it tributary to
their growing
                in imitation
of a disease they have not yet
witted and remedied because
they do not know to check themselves
having fouled in Siberia
and Poland and now leave the job
to deity maybe nature
    but they
are the tumor on earth
and their own remedy the name
of which you do not enounce when
you walk along the river in
a hat telling them it is made
of dried-out holy leaf
              not straw
so maybe you are a palmer

CHELAN

you were serious about the merry-go-round
at the unraked beach of the reservoir though you
might have run to the mountain too
    the one that you
could see in both water and sky if you had known
what to do with it in the morning

                 morning and
the morning and your morning were there in the smell
of a human lagoon beyond a proctor hill
and your vocabulary
    an any time to
the child you happened to be at the head start of
a serious go-round that would end in your night

RECLINATION

she began a tomato or few in
a window solarium that lightened
the room and made it more unfree during
late winter
    who might have created an
orangerie on a raw homestead up
in say the north of Alberta but had
not moved to want any home or prairie
outside the given
                her brother had done
all the running away and striding on
to wherever he could play Orion
in front of an imagined congérie
she did not need
    which let her be tied to
the unfree warm interior the more
and even with the deeper greens of June
the club chair at the window held her in

THE PLACE OF JUNE

in town the heat is beginning
to wad and if you could see it
you would remember chewn mat for
a rodent nest in the attic

the name of where you are is June
because the hum of it would not
be this park in January
nor would you have come out from town

you would like to eat fatback now
or cajole the heat away with
a frequentative call but what
you try is stick a plug in it

and the heat is beading in June
not town moreover on your chest
letting flies have at the one part
of your head you took for guarded

REPORT TO THE LOST

I ran in that garden too
                and hid
the one you tried to
        remake
on land of your own
                where they
would never find you

I remember unkept time
                in the
original one
        a cracked
wood stool nobody
                ever
thought to use or move

in your remaking there was
                garlic
which drew the stolid
        to where
you hid and they let
                you out
of never to now

I am writing a report
on a
poem and not a
poem
and your garden has
become
a reported one

FOREGROUND

my hometown is a widening
of river woods on the prairie
the breadth of which I can enjoy
in winter
                   at the year's midday
it is a city of foreground
meaning wren and heat and black shade
under tree and hedge when linden
are in flower
      I can enjoy
it now even though the prairie
is neither there nor here knowing
the town was never a tour stop
and cannot be seen in July

FROM SIDEWALKING TO A WALK

the young Asian woman that walked
into me downtown
      not unaware
would not have out of company and
they were giggling
             but here on prairie
I am not in anyone's lee with
no one in mine and can listen to
insect and bird
      the midsummertime
walking where I of the biped kind
enjoy prelacy and I own it
at one-thirty
             would at two o'clock
even were I inanimate like
the part-shell part-turtle I find in
a wagon track
      had come in the way
of a man wheel
             because other men
would dray me off and turn the turtle
over to the place

      I want to read
the part-design on the broken shell

and never the eyes of anyone
in a crowd
                get out of that leeway
go over to the prairie by foot

TRUTH IN SAN FRANCISCO

I knew that I was foreign
    not who
in a town of talkative gargoyles
but ungothic light where no one had
to wait to meet Punchinello e
Giuditta on the stage of park or
avenue nor Ferlinghetti and
Duncan
            Brautigan
    each a walking
overstatement with cap and bells to
the eye of an other

          in the name
of what I saw the troupers that way
who knew but reading them did not make
me want to get onto the platform
    only to stay
a foreigner and
not fake a twitch of aporia
in lingo not my own at an all-
night graisserie

         the town offered me
a ticket to midway make-belief

but it was not round-trip so I took
the next boat to the Farallones

RAPTURE

sundown on the great water may be
too red at a certain time to come
or have unwarranted beauty and
the sand of Lima or Mumbai or
even a beach in Oregon will
show it
                    a variety of reds
not one and taking up more high sky
than expected not going away
at the right point
        and *they are burning*
again no one will have to remark
knowing the color as smudge and of
their ordination to fire trees
in Kamčatka and Amapá to
smother the whole planet
                    and get out
at last
        climb a tower of red smoke
to another not so living one

RELEASE

were you a mind in the amnion
a day before you got out and did
you have a memory
          of drumfire
at Sedan maybe or of gorging
on carrion and as a mind in
the dark wet you would have been looking
ahead too
     hoping or not wanting
to find another mate like the one
you took in the chicken coop or the
entourage of Perón
         and what were
you dreaming if you had never run
on earth and rerun the memories

EVERY STOP BUT ONE

I do my summer rounds on
the prairie in afternoon
and I make every stop
but one
        revisiting a
gallery woods and driving
through a fit of rain and wind
to the sunlit town along
my river
    and the graveyard
on its mud bank where I would
not have to read all the names
but do
        and a hard next mile
to the farmstead of childhood
that others hold the deed to
    may efface

      but I neither
turn in nor go in the ditch
with a fist between my teeth

THE ONLY WORD

and I am going through a village
of quiet expectancy and I
do not stop to hear its word for me
and what I drive
    what I am wanting
and there is only one and the hot
white sky might be a milting pond but
I am in north woods now that would look
prelapsarian
 would even be
if I did not have to meet a truck
and know they were logging Eden one
more time
    if I did not understand
the eviction note and even so
I am walking on a trail through some
aboriginal green and waiting
for what I want by a lake of geese
at sundown
 red and white pine around
the due full moon coming up later
to a hush of wind in the aspen
but I am going through a village
of quiet expectancy
    the now
or next morning and what I wanted

I have not lacked and who are watching
to pin a word on me have it too
in their weary lapsarian way

IN PUBLIC

getting on to midnight Saturday
you can hear it if you live downtown
have a window open
    a woman's
scream of drunken mirth
        the fake glee in
a man or boy's shout-out that does not
relay any word you know and you
are listening to the very sound
of your own American mating
in the bygone
    a dated summer
and if you keep the window open
a time may come back rank when you brayed
like a pinniped too
        smelt skin or
beer on another and tried for it

but overhearing is all you get
and want from a night that you would not
reenter
    will not go rut-eyed on
the street in it again and bellow

WITHOUT CEREMONY

do not await a horn to summon you
and the many or all to put away
the dealings of human night and gather
at the meadow
           when you walk out into
a new simplicity of morning there
will be a jubilee of one and you
will know its day
      there is no jubilee
for many or all but each of them may
take up your singing and find the road to
another meadow that is not other
         and the geranium
in your window
will be the cranesbill of the afternoon

EDWARD GOTHFRED JOHNSON

1881–1940

FIRST COUSIN TWICE REMOVED

to one youngling of the homestead
in prairie cornucopia
the train horn was a morning call
to Samar and Mindanao
and a thicket of bolomen
where he would torch and kill under
a bundok

    the other children
of the homestead heard a wailing
and a reach of night but to him
it was and would be the morning
would call him home again to drive
that iron buffalo and sound
a bugle at every gate
of the line

      now crab apples have
begun to redden and drop on
his prairie cornucopia
too early in the dog days for
a burnishing or tarnishing
and the horn that drew him out is
on the track of Aguinaldo

A CARD FROM THE SHEYENNE

I did not see late summer begin
where I happened to look in the woods
over a valley
                where I could move
but not time or a time with a bird
or two that seemed to have flown rather
than fly
      with a dry trail and months' heat
in creek water and the grass around
where I could tell it by the nature
of sunlight on aspen and between
                moving no more
than I did not to
undo the inaction of the day

INTO ACCOUNT

I could write in detail about
the east end of the slough at what
was home one time
            the draining out
through a field and to the river
where my jerry-built raft had gone
one time on its own
      never found
not even when the course got dry

I am toward the east end of
a pinballing existence now
and do not look for things that went
but at what is
            at that gull on
a buoy in the richening light
of one dog day as it happens
to be
      huge lake water around
and at the high land over there
I mean to walk on and enjoy

AT THE FORT

the river woods were of Indian
and mosquito and of musketry
in eighteen sixty-two
             the prairie
stockade was of cavalrymen and
the west wind and of their cannonry

the river woods are of mosquito
and heat and adhering quiet
in two thousand and twelve
             the rebuilt
stockade is not of men or women
or the museum but of west wind

a cannonball in the river woods
a musket ball in the prairie dirt
to be found another time
             not now

SAINT GILES' AND THE MORROW

ONE

the south wind moving heat into town
and through had field dust and dirt to it
but what kept on that night
    no weaker
            no less dry
turned cool and brought a scent
of live ragweed and a memory
of ivy patches with it

    the wind
would go to an end out there or come
begin again
            nothing is over

TWO

I had been at the première of
the wind in cottonwoods and
had listened to the tape but
I would not need to get the
remastered version

                    after
sitting on the river bank
where I had first heard it and
attending the première all
over again
                    the very
crackle and waver of light
on leaf I had taken in
whenever it was and where
I needed to be and am

IT FIGURED

what I saw downtown on the plaza
was leaf or wing

what I saw come around from a tree
was either one

either dropping or flying around
maybe neither

and my eye ran after to catch it
the wing or leaf

leaf may not be wing of any bird
in the downtown

wing may not be leaf of any tree
on the plaza

what I saw downtown on the plaza
was butterfly

NINE-SEVEN-TWELVE IN TOWN

I have the exorability
to hear a drunken panhandler out
and give neither money nor a hand
but this afternoon I ignored one
and went my way to the river and
got to see a blue heron without
prearrangement
     what or who had made
it take wing I could have imagined
not known so I watched it circling on
and on and returning to the weeds
of the bank and did not think too hard

       it was a day
to stand high in like
one basswood of a kind in the sun
and let the wieldy words go around

NORTHERN PARKS

if I were orphaned to this parkland of aspen
and oak I would not hurt or dread anomaly
but see freedom I never knew among the gone
and run to meet and be of it
                    not having to
remember the name I carry to knotty age
because north is another direction and what
I find among blooming aster and goldenrod
is pertinent
        every bible camp that might
have taken me in has a driveway but only
on the edge of here and if I were granted to
this parkland now I would not turn around and look

OLD MILL

I have to remember the name
of him Lars Larsson for the pine
he brought out of the old country
to the new

          I see yellow trunk
and needle that would not have grown
at a mill or millstone
      would have
at kvarn och kvarnsten which he put
on the riverbank with a hut
for American renaming

the millstone now on dry mown turf
had kept grinding after his day
in time quitting after its own
to be relic
             and what he brought
as seed out of the old country
thrive here as American trees
with yellow trunk and perked needle
in a not-too-different north

THE NEW WORLD

I am kneeling in the dirt
at the gate to wilderness
and rise with a pinch of it
and feel my animal right
to range in the open day
but *instead of what* will have
to remain the one question

I am drunk on sun and air
and want to croon a beguine
or other song about my
new right to live animal
and die untreated but *why
for whom* and *instead of* will
have to remain the question

FARMHOUSE

the grandmother at the east window
looked out in winter and could see dawn
beyond the grove
             the white slough and field
   her birth home a quarter mile away
even to the river and even
the old country of her mind as sun
arrived from it
             the grandmother at
the east window looked out in morning
and saw May in the grove
    at its foot
her hollyhock bed and some dewed lawn
and thought what she would have to water
and tend that day of the sun's giving
          how it all
    might have been different
and was not

          there is no grandmother
at the window and no granddaughter
in wait at the south one now with all
having been
    I look out anyway
on a winter white and a May green

from an east room that my mind will not
abandon
                nothing is different

RIDDLING IN SEPTEMBER

my people were an other
that came and settled it here

and what did their teachings say
about a fallen acorn

to watch a box-elder bug
would have seemed undue to them

and I've seen one on a tree
turn into many flying

the way I am up and on
may be mine or not because

there are no other people
and there is no kabbalah

AUTUMN WATCH

the cameras and the wind had left
and red maple seemed to withdraw to
a silence that invited

here was
evening without color for all
but the pilgrims were gone and I would
be taking it in alone
                    counting
the hoots of a great gray and watching
a moon that was one night out of full
make zenith

the tables had no one
at them and the dried-up public grass
could not unbend and I heard a leaf
on my tent sometime

but red maple
would be out in the morning for me

Other Middle Island Press titles by Rodney Nelson are available via Amazon.com and the Middle Island Press website.

Felton Prairie (2014)

ISBN 978-0-6922-6780-6

Fargo (2014)

ISBN 978-1-4951-0352-0

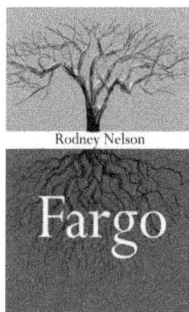

Sighting the Flood (2013)

ISBN 978-1-4675-7626-0

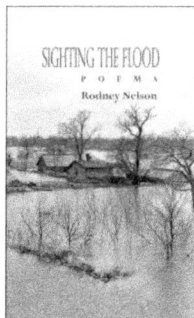

Bog Light (2013)

ISBN 978-1-4675-6739-8

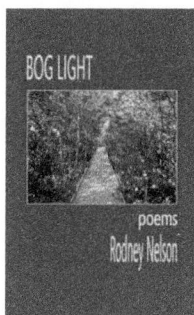

www.ingramcontent.com/pod-product-compliance
Lightning Source LLC
Chambersburg PA
CBHW030926090426
42737CB00007B/336